I0623375

Collected Poems

WALLACE BARKER

MAXIMUS BOOKS
NORTH · FLORIDA
2023

Copyright © 2023 by Wallace Barker

ISBN: 979-8-9868347-1-9 (paperback)

Published by Maximus Books in the USA
First edition

This book is about life with my family, Alicia, Esmé and Miles. They are my inspiration and my hope.

Acknowledgments

Steff Duhem helped curate this collection, sorting through a mountain of poems to select the ones presented here, and she also suggested the structure. The encouragement and collaboration of my editor, Hayden Church, are the reasons this book exists at all. I also want to thank my longtime confidante and great friend, Paul Hanson Clark, for endless discussions about poetry and everything else. Steff, Hayden and Paul are my favorite poets – their support has been a defibrillator whenever the heart of my practice begins to fail, and I think every artist needs that.

The following poems first appeared in the literary journals and magazines indicated below.

'She Judged Petals in Disarray' first appeared in *22nd Century Literature*;
'Origami City,' 'Peaceful Easy Feeling,' 'You Can Count on Me,' and 'Wild Life' first appeared in *Back Patio Press*;
'Marital Rites' and 'The Savior and the Saved' first appeared in *Banango Street*;
'Never Again Will The Waters Become a Flood' and 'An Education' first appeared in *Curbside Splendor*;
'Rebel Rebel' first appeared in *The Curiosity Cabinet*;
'Transfer Request' and 'Supercell' first appeared in *The Daily Drunk*;
'Levelland' first appeared in *Electric Cereal*;
'The Wild God of the World' and 'Six Seeds' first appeared in *Expat Press*;
'I Feel Like a Young Babe Ruth' and 'Eating a Pretty Good Salad at Your Desk' first appeared in *Fluland*;

'I Still Have Not Quit Smoking,' 'Young Once Only,' 'Poet's Younger Brother,' and 'Massacre' first appeared in *Have U Seen My Whale*;

'If the Birds Take Flight,' 'Next Year's Glossy Magazines,' and 'Drunk Dials at 330am I Love Them' first appeared in *Keep This Bag Away From Children*;

'Last Swim at Roberta's House' first appeared in *LIEF+*;

'Day Drinking' and 'Amazon Prime Day' first appeared in *Misery Tourism*;

'Force Majeure' first appeared in *Moonlight Mag*;

'Saturn's Rings' and 'The Reunion' first appeared in *Nauseated Drive*;

'i am pretending to be a mayfly,' 'March and April,' 'Alicia,' and 'Au Revoir Les Enfants' first appeared in *Neutral Spaces Magazine*;

'Chrysanthemums' and 'To Anyone Who Ever Had a Heart' first appeared in *No Lotus*;

'Anxiety Attacks and the Drugs That Fix Them' first appeared in *Philosophical Idiot*;

'Fox News' and 'Alice' first appeared in *Purple Pig Lit*;

'Night Storm' first appeared in *Reality Hands*;

'Not Abt That Life' first appeared in *The Scrambler*;

'Incommunicado' first appeared in *Screaming Seahorse*;

'The Farthest Mosque,' 'Gucci Linens,' and 'Prayer to a Tiny African God' first appeared in *Soft Cartel*;

'Marriage Vacation' first appeared in *Thousand Shades of Gray*;

'New Year 2016' first appeared in *Uncle Ken Presents*;

'The Real World' and 'Reverse Photosynthesis' first appeared in *Weird Laburnum*;

'Put Yourself in my Position' first appeared in *The Wondrous Real Magazine*;

'The Good Samaritan' first appeared in *Words & Sports Quarterly*
'Salvator Mundi' first appeared in *YAWP*.

CAPULET

God's bread, it makes me mad.
Day, night, hour, tide, time, work, play...

(*Romeo and Juliet*, 3.5.187–188)

CONTENTS

1 *Work*

Transfer Request

I put in a request for a transfer because
the local office was getting to be a downer.
I filled out the requisite form to ask

if they would transfer me to the Alhambra
I made extravagant promises – I would definitely
create a proof of the Riemann Hypothesis and achieve cold fusion

I signed my name on the form "Extra Careful"
tied the transfer form to the leg of a cow with red ribbon
and clipped the barbed wire fence so she might run free.

I painted my eyelids black and performed chants
in my living room that I learned from the 14 year old
Satan worshipper next door.

I drove to the FedEx/Kinkos store and
mailed several sketches of the cloudless sky
to the Dalai Lama.

I am still waiting for a response from the HR Dept.
day after day in my house with no lights on
shades drawn to cover the windows

memorizing all the stars in the universe
in preparation for my journey.

If the Birds Take Flight

Ecstatic when you offered me
your gatorade on the street corner
sunrise strung out and my mouth was parched
from smoking cigarettes all night
bums stirring in lean-tos
packing sleeping bags to trek the city.

Cartwheeling heart when we slid down the embankment
because the maintenance crew called to us
as we were smoking a joint.

Small hum in my ears from the lowlit dash
in the nighttime on a road trip
to recover your car from police impound
dreaming of breakfast platters.

Gone, spent, blissed as a seer
errant highways, house parties, pastures and ranch roads
savages and we sensed savagely
though never noticed our path led
into some long and boring ambush.

Picnic Lunch

early winter wearing red socks
in cold sun and dry grass crunching
beneath boots all the spinning clouds
and birds winging down the jetstreams

emails buzzing in my pocket
seem to cry in agony against my thigh
as if i were a deaf god leaving
the faithful to their dumb fates

and so i am a deaf god walking on
a gravel path to the picnic table in the park
when the sun goes behind a cloud the wind is cold
but i don't care…it won't kill me

text messages, status updates, social media
spinning around low earth orbit at
speeds that are beyond understanding
and me, the god of ignorance, of sloth

of disregard, of inattentiveness
my conscience is stored away
carefully secured from tiresome prayers
i am sitting at a picnic table unwrapping my sandwich

i am looking at red and gold leaves

i am far away from any ministrations

The Capital of the Heart of the World

Nothing was easy as they made it out to be
awkward as a baby giraffe I struggled to find
my purchase somehow accomplish feats that
seemed cruelly simple for most the heavy

summer hot town boiling concrete gives way to
green hill country all those people nestled in
the hills living in great mansions and me down
below commuting from one disaster to the next

all those superior intellects cruising Congress Avenue
in tailored suits tan leather shoes walking
in wide arcs around the homeless who lay
on the sidewalk in rags newspapers body fluids

at the heart of the galaxy is a black hole
we are all circling the drain in this regard
the range rovers waiting in the valet line
the man I knew who shot and killed a cabbie

and then was killed by the police and the man
who worked in my office as an intellectual property
litigator his body was atrophied when I met him
from multiple brain surgeries meant to excise a tumor.

Sinecure

Outflows are exceeding the inflows
the ledger is entirely off I left
work with an infected tooth

the light fixtures are separating from the ceiling
dark as the shadow across the great ledger
we have been found to be insolvent

so it feels like ethics don't really exist
morality is a luxury the limestone hills
roll off toward the suspension bridge

yoked across the colorado river knifing
the hill country splitting all the accounts
reminding us that everything requires payment

and the goal as always is to stand beside that river
and divert some little channel for yourself.

Welcome to the Fiberhood

the phone dropped in water fizzled
dark screen reflects a blinking visage
night terrors reaching for a connection
no longer there and everyone sending impotent

messages to me the spacewalker unmoored
and floating slowly away from the planet
missing details like political conventions
mass shootings and a pretty damn hot selfie

from some brainy cultural journalist then also
work emails confused clients even the tree leaves
blowing outside the window waving frantically
batting out some snide morse code comment on the

thinkpiece of my life alone from humanity no meme
no show no input whatsoever and the course of some
lit cigarette from hand to mouth hot and burning
in the evening its monstrous energy levels able

to power any number of electronic devices probably
probably this salmon dinner this globe fallen over
this sweet lady whispering my name my horrified family

waving waving

I'm drifting into some indifferent waters now

Anxiety Attacks and the Drugs That Fix Them

always hard to understand that literally
nothing is sustainable the best that can
be done is a temporary improvement
critics of orion in the sky his phallic belt

swinging over the horizon the master of that
entrance when the city lights are far enough
away to see stars for once then you can see space
traumas from the working world dissolve against

your forehead close your eyes the night cow moans
space astronauts would come to this world and laugh
at all the unnecessary hardship the dirt drying out
the pawns moving one square at a time dust everywhere

I thought about Susan on her bean bag chair laughing
at my anxiety fit her long legs curled up her tights
with some kind of space pattern some dyed nebula
purple splotch her tightly closed eyes her laughing

The Only Chance I Have

Two people I went to highschool with
died in the same week one from cancer
the other shot by police after he went on

a shooting rampage in a hotel lobby killing
a sixty year old cab driver death is upon
my graduating class on the news they said

a "man" shot the cab driver and I was surprised
that they didn't say he was a kid but of course
he's not a kid none of us are kids anymore

planet earth kept rotating around a nuclear fireball
and now we are men and soon we will be old men
the moss growing on rocks in my backyard

may one day overtake them entirely
what will that mean what will have changed
this oak growing up through a hole in the deck

will thicken and split the deck the ivy growing
on the south wall will climb to the rooftop
earth's rotation is slowing each year
and the laws of physics will bury me deep.

Divertissement

happy to be leaving work elated really
skipping the staircase down into 92 degree
hot sunlight along the bleached concrete
path to the bleached concrete monolith

up another staircase to my parked car and saw
the treetops sway just below the parking garage
fourth level and drove my car directly across
the highway to a supermarket to get

a six pack of pilsner beer and took only
surface streets home tho I know the drive
is longer that way it seems like I would never
go to work again tomorrow might as well be

the sun going cold or tectonic plates springing
against one another joyfully washing all
the useless business away the carpeted hallways
and computerized tasks repetitive dull

the sky as white with heat as the sidewalk
then radiating that heat even in cool night
when across west texas plains sagebrush
rattled and further still toward the brown

arizona desert where the night creatures
were just beginning their shifts

Prayer to a Tiny African God

lit screen mischief that kind of thing
tweeting some far out shit or leaving cynical
comments on someone's FB post what a joke

the ice skating rink at whole foods in the winter
sometimes the ice gets a little too carved up
seems a bit slushy really but I love the warm

chocolate smell of that place though the misery
of people living on downtown streets in America
is overwhelming they ask for money and I walk by

but I am not a monster at least I hope not
the broken granite paving and boarded up shop
windows the hard luck homeless what deep and

unfathomable well of abuse left them stranded
this way the night air as evening sets in the violet
sunset crown over the city the high road pool

with its skyline views and watery margaritas
the earth is cruel because nature is cruel some mystery
left me in this world and overhead some entirely different universe

Only the Interesting Things

she cant offer anything to anyone
and never claimed she would
seems absurd that even in miserable
cold weather she might be expected to
contribute something beyond

what she loved best like novels by Ursula K. Leguin
and the paintings in museums by artists without
famous names neglected on the wall

finding a pressed flower in a book
so much human life was not interesting
it seemed amazing to her humans

ordered their affairs in this way and yes yes
she understood about the capitalist patriarchy
and why society might be structured so

but how awful to even think about those things
politics, like war, seemed a sure sign
nothing interesting would ever happen again

Eating a Pretty Good Salad at Your Desk

I think abt James who was the editor in chief
of the college journal and his late nights
in the office at such a young age we were all

just experimenting with being adults I guess
but he looked worn and balding tho he wasn't old
stress at any age is nothing to brag abt I suppose

night dancing in your underwear the symphony
balcony seats the jug of wine that can outlast
poor James with his temples throbbing at his desk

propriety and all that miserable squalor button ups
and choking interactions with older ppl who have
secret and pointless money ambitions that pollute

your knowledge of them your tobacco scented cologne
from the yucatan city of valladolid mexico the weird
fact of dreary parts of life that denial of magic

hopeless in office trousers hopeless staring at computers
hopeless watching political debates hopeless liking
political memes on social media the damn scent of electrical

fire in your brain miswired the tulips growing in a landscaped
office park all those shrill harmonies and you moaning
your baritone thinking it's a protest but really

it's only the bass line.

West 6th Street and Colorado

Ephedrine dream that would spill orange
laced ravings into my life where I was only
trying to reach some kind of equilibrium

banana colored pills, strawberry colored pills
drank an entire bottle of wine and the whole
time I was thinking about getting more wine.

Read only a few lines of a book before
forgetting where I left it bookshelf is empty
some kind of lettering on the walls seems

to be an inspirational message about the importance
of family the unspoken context of course is imminent
death disaster betrayal old age and decrepitude.

I saw the most beautiful girl I had ever seen
waiting tables at a sushi restaurant and it felt embarrassing
because everyone was pretending they didn't care.

My friend offered me a hit from some kind of vaporizer
that looked like an early ipod I smoked and it tasted
like hot electrical wires and this is supposed to be better

than burning a jay seems like I have crossed a line
age...I don't know...but all my passions are so confusing.

I Feel Like a Young Babe Ruth

remembered at work that its actually a big universe
of things you could be choosing to do but I dont know
here we are tweeting abt political conventions again

and outside it seems the trees have grown too thick
the shade has killed off all the grass I saw a pretty
lady but didnt bother to look really bc even tho

possibilities are endless you have to admit this seems kinda
inapplicable or theoretical at best I was reading one of those
french books that always have to mention the name of every

street like rue de jacques or whatever I made that one up
but you understand you can get how I was at work
it felt a little bizarre to be staring at simulated

screen stuff the pretty lady and the shaded patch outside hot
sun and thai ice cream vendor by the pool everyone is choosing
basically where they want to be at that moment and this decision

determines everything I have heard some ppl say when
you see a cardinal its an omen of death but I love a red
cardinal clearing all the branches overhead

Starry Eyes What Could I Say or Do?

thinking hard on the walk back to her apartment
like Darwin trying to puzzle "why things are the way
that they are" this question about actions and reactions

sometimes she thought it seemed like physical science
because gravity exerts X force and because Y properties
of thermodynamics function in a certain way it was always

inevitable that she would be getting older in an overpriced
city apartment with plenty of friends and lovers not as if
she were some lonely person but still like a scoop of ice cream

she could topple off her cone at any moment and people would
be disappointed maybe even sad but life would continue
without too much interruption and then other times

it didn't seem scientific at all it seemed much more
vague and nuanced there were things that were said
at different points and she reacted in instinctive ways

others took offense or sometimes did not and things pinballed
wildly in erratic directions the streetlamps were winking
on and so night was just beginning the air felt colder

as she walked and the sky darkened it felt very much
like she was traveling into space the streets were emptied
all the oxygen was emptying out and she was floating slowly

into the arms of orion walking together now
into a more permanent constellation.

An Education

Mopping the floor smelled sour
perhaps the water was old
late shift winding down
fluorescent lights bright cold.

I went to check the bathroom
the mess I'd have to clean
it smoked with wispy fumes
faintly gasoline.

I did not open the door
but turned and mopped right back
because I knew inside
my boss was smoking crack.

Unsure but sure not scared
even at sixteen
working the convenience store
it wasn't the craziest thing I had seen.

Incommunicado

I called you on your cell phone but you hung up
you said the signal dropped there was static
on the line the cell phone towers
were in revolt the landline was decrepit
emails all bounced from the server
I couldn't find you on the internet

you told me the possibility of human communication
was diminishing from the earth
you put on a coat and walked out the door
it was so cold I almost didn't follow
the streets were iced and I slid in my loafers
looking in windows of closed coffee shops and shuttered dress
    boutiques

I saw you from across the street and tried to wave
but the fog was too thick – you didn't see me
I ran toward you into the road
and was struck by a car

you craned over my body
looked down into my eyes and I was dazed
saw your blurry visage descending ever closer
as I fell backwards into a long dark tunnel

The Savior and the Saved

I was too distracted to notice the
flowers in you hair when I arrived
and your slender wrist
circled by a thin gold band

the landlord told me your rent was past due
you would soon be evicted
he was demanding recompense
as though I were your father
I gave him the $200 I had in my wallet
and he said you could stay until next Tuesday

natural light pouring in from the long windows
blazing hot afternoon outside but in the empty space
indoors the air was cool and a ceiling fan turned the breeze
there seemed to be no furniture
though you had been living there for years

thin cotton blouse against
your dark brown skin you thanked me
offered a lemonade and a shot of gin
nowhere to sit
I held the sweating glass tight
and felt dizzy from the alcohol rush

Madeline, it was the last thing I remember
tiny gray birds flitting past the bare windows
shock of white sunlight across the blond wood floor
your green eyes watching me drink

and though I had come to take you away from all this
it was you who redeemed me from the wasted avenues

Marital Rites

Upon arrival I took my handbag down
shouldered it and walked the plane aisle
loitering in the airport pigeons
mere birds
left shoeless by the baggage cart
midnight with the arrivals and departures screen flickering
waiting on a late night flight
we were both so tired.

Strangers, we were not embarrassed to be seen by one another
fully dressed trying to sleep
without blankets on an airport bench.

It was more intimate
than obvious encounters I felt
as if we had been married for years
and sleeping together this way.

Me with my socks on knees curled under
you with a purse for a pillow.

Saturn's Rings

i think there are probably ppl floating
in space right now maybe in the space station

imagine those ppl and here i am starting another work week
it's only monday but i'm procrastinating about leaving the house

i don't want to go to work of course
i would be just fine in the space station

i would read books and write little poems like this one
i've seen so many mourning doves lately

it was a bumper crop this year because i guess
it has been raining more than usual

and the squirrels too have multiplied they are rampant
in the parks and their dead bodies litter the roads

i hold all of this in my orbit
my immense gravity causes this menagerie

to circle me and circle me and circle me

Walk Away From Trouble If You Can

things are tough all over my dad used to say
in response to almost any complaint always
eyes toward the horizon as if speaking to himself
as if he was considering some anonymous struggle.

I read today that a wealthy oil executive
drove his car at high speed directly
into a wall and it exploded and he died
after learning he was under indictment.

He didn't think a head-on collision with a wall
was as bad as legal troubles the world continued
to turn anyway who mourns that guy in some sense
it seems impossible to feel too bad for a guy like that.

Some people have a better chance of keeping their money
not getting into legal trouble over whatever happened
the haze of history often fogs over bad decisions
always slamming into some wall at great speeds.

Armies have truly perished in avoidable circumstances
it's amazing to think of the sun spasming in the sky
during some long march a black mist covering your eyes
covering your face washing you and all your friends

into the forgotten dimension.

When This Yokel Comes Maundering

At the height of his popularity
he was often mistaken
for someone who had important things to say.

Like all great artists
he had to hit the road
you can't write about Indiana forever.

To struggle against its current
then converge onto arterial superhighways
as a salmon returns to breeding grounds.

Until he was standing in shadows of tall buildings
beautiful women strolled the sidewalks.

Women who had they been so walking
in Indiana would have been royalty
"Oh yes," he thought, "now I see."

"These killers have really
made a home for themselves."

No Moon Only a Space Station

The last attempt and also the worst
the audience sort of backing away
meandering off one at a time then

later in the dressing room tears
recriminations the night outside
empty as a clamshell on the beach

Christine cleaned herself up and started walking
thought about calling a driver but wanted
to punish herself in some way with

this long walk back to her apartment
or maybe nothing quite so harsh as that
but just wanted to give all the steam

time to dissipate from behind her eyeballs
life would often be like this you prepare
you try but the balloon deflates and falls

the audience is politely embarrassed
to watch any further she could see a lit
convenience store sign bright in the sky

it felt obscene she walked toward it toward
some terrible bottle of wine she would purchase
to stain her teeth blue to open her up again toward

that crucial illusion of a quiet mind.

Lucky Weather Patterns

all the whistle stop adventure tours
affluent professionals and their blonde
children skiing slopes and storming beaches
thoroughly documented on social media

surely this is nothing to be upset about
think of the dying grandparents the shadow
across a lung the night when your adult sister
had a mental crack-up and was taken to the

asylum to begin a new antipsychotics regimen
the raccoon split open in the road as you drive
to work in the morning the cruelties at both ends

of the rainbow

The Good Samaritan

yesterday I was playing golf with my friend
and we heard moaning sounds from bushes
near a railroad track on the outskirts of the course

at first I just continued my game thinking it was
probably not anything or maybe some tramps
fighting or taking drugs or something

but I could picture myself from an outside view
playing golf while someone died in the bushes
so I went to investigate and found two tramps

a man and a woman smoking cigarettes
I asked if they were ok and they laughed
the man said "are you ok Julie?" and she laughed

and gave me a thumbs up
I think they were having sex back there.

Heaven Isn't Too Far Away

Cara was not impressed and that was how
things had been for quite some time there were
rainstorms and then the sidewalk smelled strongly

of ozone hot steam sometimes coming off the concrete.
Sure people sent emails about work projects or whatever
ephemera was occupying them at the moment but

none of it was substantial or lasting in any way everything
was the future bird cage lining sunsets even were accompanied
by closing credits or something awful like that the unbearable

heartbreak when she was driving down main street and saw
a beautiful woman pushing an expensive high-end stroller
conspiring against her happiness as hyenas may stalk and kill

a lioness as the great plains and jungles are home
to murderous intent inky night where little egg robbers
roam trying to kill babies darting abhorrent lizards

with egg teeth and swampy noises everywhere she left the
dive bar where once she saw attractively louche strangers
now she saw dirtbags dangerous enemies even she rode

her bike home in the night happy to speed by walking people
flying past streetlights, streetlamps, streetlights.

Origami City

heading back to work on a cold and sunny day
ive earned a living my entire life now i support

plenty of other people i drive to the office
spend 8 or 10 hours frustrated and cross

then drive back home at night often eat dinner
alone that i have warmed up in the microwave

i know about quiet desperation but i also know
about real desperation because i have driven beneath

the overpass and seen the homeless encampment there
the city folds over onto itself and some people

are crushed that way and some people navigate
the creases over and over even as the folding

leaves a smaller and smaller page

All the Assholes in the World and Mine

she was moving closer but
purposeless unsure what might
result from the proximity and
ultimately gave up on her plan

just sitting a bit too close to him
but not close enough to suggest
anything other than awkwardness

maybe he could sense her longing
but probably not because humans
mostly don't pay attention to eachother

unless money or sex is a possibility
and she knew she wasn't really offering
either on the ferry traveling across

grey morning waters because what would
that even look like or who has time
for anything really everything is so

exhausting she couldn't catch his eye
because he was reading a handheld device
she stood and imagined falling into the water

she wouldn't have to go to work if that happened

Bad Name

bees construct hives from the inside out
a beehive is a material expression
of the thoughts of bees

on a cold night
exhalations hung in the air
wind stirred
what was the story
in that dank courtyard

it was the palpable dark
it was semiconductors
and powerless flat screens
unilluminated purgatory
my mind was abscessed

I wore shiny shoes and cut my hair short
there was a girl who seemed to prefer cardigans
and we were all growing older in the same place
I thought maybe I should get a degree or something

on a bitter cold night
we were confused when
all the street lamps blinked at once

Peaceful Easy Feeling

I was very drunk at a martini party
sitting around the fire pit with some
young successful tech bros and lawyers

my friend gave me a vape pen with
indica weed when I first arrived and
I was stoned losing my grip.

These guys were talking at me about
something but the fire was so warm
I couldn't really respond and I thought my

normal thoughts about being overwhelmed
and possibly inferior and then you arrived
Alicia in your green dress and black boots

with your bangs falling across your glasses
and I liked that so much I like you so much
you seemed very cool to me.

I told the guys around the fire that you
are my wife in an interrupting manner and
I felt very glad and self-assured about you.

That made me calm and strong in my thoughts.
The fire was indeed warm so I sat back and
you talked and made everyone laugh.

Order in the Universe

I was so tired the wine wouldn't
do it for me anymore
leather chair
red light from frosted glass
could feel my hair disheveled
appreciative that the physical world
always reflects the mental

and of course each manifestation
is more broadly metaphorical
your mind
the disorganized room
the hairy planet
expanding star cluster

appollonian
the planets do rotate
precisely in their orbits

Day Drinking

I was drinking all day and all night
playing golf with beers in the cool morning
then a lunch of cheeseburgers and more beer

afterward on the porch with friends i smoked
a joint and drank more beers then ate an edible
marijuana gummy and had several glasses of wine

with dinner only to stay up late by myself after
everyone else had gone to bed and I drank tequila
with sparkling water while watching fight videos on youtube.

In the morning I woke heavy but it felt a bit pleasant
maybe not so different from how one feels
the morning after a hard workout like I had

really outdone myself but black stones gathered
around my neck as the leaden hours dissolved into day.
Soon I was marched to the rotting bridge over the moor

and sunk to the bottom of the marsh to drown and die.

Massacre

My purpose was wrong-footed
first the short days of winter
then the surprise of vernal equinox
driving a four-wheeler practicing jumps
on a dirt mound.

When all at once my youth
was spent at the swollen lake
wading into murky water
I stood on a submerged car.

We were rolling joints
from textbook pages waiting out the flood
you were building a fire along the riverbank.

We played guitar and as it got later
stole beer from a corner store.

Now flummoxed by carpeted hallways
and row upon row of filing cabinets
I'm afraid I've forgotten a crucial point.

Once we were bold as raccoons
the sun was warm I floated
the overgrown river and felt my belly swell.

Time put an end to all that
we were marched to an abandoned
building and lined against the wall

I was the first to be shot
now it is your job to haul my body
into the mass grave
then you will be shot.

2   *Nature*

I am Pretending to be a Mayfly

The branches hang over the lake
Cutting the sky into stained glass mosaic
And the gravel spilling over the banks
Disturbed by the feet of joggers

Drops into the water thereby
Segmenting that clear plane as well.
Everything is grey and brown.
Ivy sags a rotten leaf over the fence

Through which chainlink I can see
Yoga people doing poses in the park.
Each yogi is framed by her own
Chainlink diamond and a toppled

Bicycle stripped of its front wheel
Lolls in the bushes like a crime victim.
I am here for anyone who needs me but
No one needs me and that's fine too.

I am like a bee in a honeycomb
Waxing myself into a hexagonal cell
Hoping I might emerge transformed
Into some new winged insect.

But of course

That doesn't happen for bees.

The Poet's Younger Brother

I opened a store selling stones to birds
but I would trade feathers and ribbon
to see you again.

And all the rain shaking
the cedar forests
is nothing to me
if you would come home.

These Saturday mornings
speaking Cantonese
to little children
and lazy afternoons
reading about Siberian prisons
I would gladly forsake.

I have been learning to play
Tears for Fears on my guitar
I would surely perform
most of the Songs From the Big Chair
on the day you arrive.

Never Again Will The Waters Become a Flood

Night to a faint glow
tangerine blossom horizon
downtown bars ejected patrons shivering at dawn.

Drunk and enraptured
by the earth slowly tilting toward its polestar
lit cigarettes dangled as
an automatic hand brushed hair.

This orange morning when flocks
of city birds wheeled in the sky
bisected by slack telephone wire
a dying buzz cottoned the periphery.

What glory crowned the earth!
The moon still reflected in skyscraper glass
last stars winking into transitional light
how could this portend daytime recriminations?

As if the covenant between god and man were reversed
and the coming of the great flood
prefigured by a cruel promise of hope.

The Wild God of the World

I saw a hawk stoop in the sky and dive down below the treeline.
I saw two hawks playing in the sky as I stood in front of my
    brother's grave.
I look for hawks everywhere and at the cemetery
I see them more often than you might think.

One time in Sante Fe I saw a hawk attempt to hit a dove
Sitting on a tree branch and it was like an explosion in the tree.
But the dove escaped with the hawk in pursuit.
Everywhere was high desert and brown mountains.

I read that young hawks begin by playing with other birds.
They find flocks of birds in the sky and swoop with them
Just doing acrobatics in the sky and enjoying the thrill of flight
But eventually they kill one of the birds probably on accident

Because their talons are sharp and they fly with such velocity.
This first playful kill becomes the basis for a lifetime of hunting.
They learn and are perhaps surprised to find they are not playing
And it was never a game and the entire world turns on its axis

To face the sun and then away from the sun
Forever and ever as far as any of us are concerned.

Supercell

Late night at our campsite
the children asleep in their tents
James passed out in the grass
I played Cure songs on my guitar.

The air felt charged with ions
prickling across my neck
gusts clattered gear off the picnic table.

Heat lightning arced across the sky
followed by reverberating thunder
nervous conversations stopped
eyes scanning the horizon.

Our fire dropped to embers
then a sharp crack and a falling branch
knocked Amity in the head
when her husband ran over to help
she shrieked like a wounded animal.

Cries from frightened children
a tarp from the neighboring site
was blown into a distant campfire
I raced through the trees toward it.

And the darkness of nature
yet boomed across the sky
savage ecstatic

take me too
sprinting into the heart

Put Yourself in my Position

i have seen the winter sun rise
over the trail surrounding the lake
light tumble down the shore breaks
a stricken man plunging to water

and laughed while my hot breath in clouds
dissipated before me and ducks paddled away
i observed graffiti beneath the concrete bridge
and imagined the lives of those nighttime writers

dodged the slow grandmothers in brimmed hats
walking three or four abreast blocking the entire
trail as frustrated bikers in stretch pants and
mirrored glasses hunt for passage around

and i ran up into the hills then back down
to the trails and the city was completely
drunk and wasted at 8am like some
hooligan day-drinker and i remembered

my boyhood and all my life in this town
i felt completely in love as Romeo upon
his first glimpse of Juliet across a crowded
party and i climbed the steep grade

back toward my little house in the sunlight
to shower and get ready for my day

Spring

did a trick on my bike
just a bunny hop actually
my foot slipped off the pedal

and the sharp teeth
gouged my shin
blood was pouring

down my leg and soaking
my green socks it was a sunny day
and i was on a gravel trail that

circles the lake in my town
i saw a mourning dove cautiously
emerge from the hedges

three turtles were sunning themselves
on a log floating in the water
almost overlapping one another

i worried other ppl on the trail
might think i was strange
biking around with a gash in my shin

blood pooling in my sock and
spilling over into my shoe so
i rode home amid all the splendor of god's creation

Wild Happiness

Clara wondered why being alone sometimes
made her feel euphoric like she had escaped
something maybe the world's clutches it felt

manic and hard to articulate lots of animals
are solitary which is not to say she wanted
to be alone all the time but that initial rush

really thrilled her she watched squirrels out
the window climbing the bare branches of fall
the soggy landscape not cold enough to freeze

those branches sectioning the sky those squirrels
oblivious to her watching it's interesting to wonder
if wild animals are happy in any way that resembles

how humans understand happiness seems equally likely
they may be terrified all the time the world is like a
grandparent that squeezes you and pinches your cheeks

asks you strange questions you can't really answer
though you do love it, you always just want to get away really.

Reality Simulation

Switchbacks up the limestone hills
the loose mud tires spraying
blue mountain bike tumble
back down to hot pavement

all the violence of passing cars
and a pretty girl jogging by
ponytail describing a figure eight
orange gaudy running shoes light

stink of decay along the lakeshore edge
like schrodinger's cat something may
be dead here but if left unseen
it can't be fixed in the classical

sense the cheap beer tallboy sweating
in the hands of a lake vagrant rolling
his bedroll for the long hike back
to whatever intersection he haunts

and then my life and my hands my eyes
I'm going past all of it on my blue
bicycle uncertain even of my own
existence as if I were a reflection

off the wavy lake surface.

March and April

grey dawn across the city when
i remember the death of my brother the artist
and his little cemetery plot in onion creek

and how he played harmonica
i see a hawk following my car down the interstate
it soars over me then dips below the hills

the morning in april when my brother was born
and the morning in march when my brother died
he was not yet 20 years old and since that morning

more years have passed
than he ever even lived but
he will forever be older than me

in my mind and of course
more intelligent and worldly
and skillful in all things

i saw a heron tiptoe through the shallow
part of the lake on this powder morning
it moved and then it was still for longer

than i could maintain focus
it seemed as if it was frozen there
and could remain so forever

completely outside time and oblivious to my aging

White Azaleas

white feathered chicken
standing on the eroded
slope the pink flowers
late blossoms

gentleman rooster lost along
the hyacinths the ivy overgrowing
late tuesday morning intervals of

thick coke bottle glasses and other eccentricities
shopping for port wine and cigarettes at the
suburban supermarket with Jane the terror

of east coast supper clubs the avenging sword
the last toke of a reduced joint on 1st street
like the challenger space shuttle

a sad fireball winking out

Science Defeats the Personal and the Impersonal

be careful when you meet ppl
bc the fantasy aint real some ppl
seem kind or fun but its not true

they are weird hypochondriacs or have
problems w their parents you cant address
and these things are not cute quirks they

might resolve but devastating life
problems that assert themselves fully
in middle age and you will be the stunned

owner of a broken life caring for broken lives
dont trust ppl dont trust the mental health
of ppl who seem normal nothing is as it seems

animals know this monkeys mate but they are
always en garde they bare their teeth even when
a loved one gets too close they know abt random

violence sadness mental instability all those
things that plague thinking creatures look at the hard
sidewalk all the ppl that live upon it all the broken

relationships of the world funneling down into
yr super concentrated broken relationship where
water birds dance and then go under drowned

first blush of something beautiful gives way to damage
that the pure physics of the universe inflicts on weak

shivering lifeforms w no protections

The Reunion

My blood feels good at night.
I don't know why, I just like it
a calm sedative when dark air

comes through the window and the TV
is on but muted. Light with no sound.
What has been made will be distributed.

Senior commentators shrug their shoulders.
Crystals form first from a seed then
grow rapidly in a fractal pattern.

The harbor seals fight on a wet wooden dock.
They all want the sunny patch drying out.
So, in this way, nuclear energy from the fireball

millions of miles away sows discord among fat sea mammals.
I did a flip off the diving board at the city pool and
my face slapped the water so hard my ears were ringing.

I swam to the side and found the last bit
of evening sun in that cold mist to
warm up a bit and dry my trunks briefly.

Cocktail Party

shuddered saw a small bird dead on
the pedestrian bridge its body quite grisly
I only zoomed past on my bike but felt

the broken promise spread out before me
then squashed by some meaningless misstep
that is why nothing is to be trusted

even a slight shift of weight can cause
damage impossible to repair life is fragile
so arbitrary but charming in the same way

that a grass blade will whistle if you cup it and
blow gently just right anything could happen!
due to mental instabilities I fell short but

I am with you in tucson where it is hot and raining
I am with you in baltimore where decay is no
obstacle and the unutterable prophecies of

hangover headaches and aspirin showers
in the morning the deep unsettled root that
will never give up sterile shopping malls

where the goddamn genius store is shuttered
they tried to sell a watch that required lots of
attention everything is so bizarre and you were

placed here like me some prank blind date to make
your way with stunned disbelief and awkward

small talk

The Real World

Blowout along the way to work
I stop on the shoulder to change the tire
cars speeding by so fast
I felt hot gusts with
the violence of their passing.

And this violent street
seemed so serene
only moments earlier as I
navigated its easy turns
in a climate-controlled environment
listening to mid-century
French crooners on my iPhone.

Now I see the edges of the road
are littered with tire scraps and shards
of shattered auto glass
a raccoon corpse bloats in the sun.

I am changing my tire quickly
harassed by speeding sideview mirrors
which seem almost to clip my shoulder
carelessly close, I curse unconcerned drivers
such an impact would surely leave me crippled.

And as I finish mounting the tire
eager to return to my former idyll
I spot a buzzard at the tree line

patiently waiting for me to die
or else leave it to the raccoon carcass.

Physics and Consequences

to all the pigeons on 10th street
the people have heard your demands
horse-faced boy in the coffee shop

knows your plight the girl skipping classes
to wander with her backpack among the towers
the cab drivers circling expensive hotels

the entrepreneurs laboring over some aspect of
the conversion funnel of their obscure websites
the salesman wears a suit and tie everyday though

such attire is long out of fashion and
abandoned by all except the desperate
he carries a worn sample case down

congress avenue the cruelties of the world
you are collateral damage pigeon no one
meant to harm you or make your life difficult

it's only the grinder that minces us all
turning its inexorable gears it's only
some obscure natural law evolving beasts

of the earth

Sturm und Drang

rental electric scooter mouldering
in the brush beside the lakeshore
maintenance crew driving golf carts
on the trail to paint over graffiti

upsetting joggers as they block the path
all the chill morning air is concentrated
here in the fading starlit morning
steam rises from the lake to dissipate

with car exhaust and shiny buildings
reach all the way into clouds such that
the building tops are entirely obscured
long-necked waterbirds prance in the shallows

they pause for long intervals looking at the water
after breakfast we pull our trashbins
to the curb there is a brown bin for
trash and a blue bin for recycling

the bins are heavy
we do not walk lightly upon the earth
we do not glide along the surface like a waterbug
hardly causing a ripple

to evade the rolling eyeball

of the silent and still egret

Salvator Mundi

All the life of the world
and how quickly it subsides.
The red-tailed hawk swooping
over the golf course is completely gone

off plastic cups of tequila
with fresh-pressed lime juice.
Completely wasted and laughing
smiling too wide and dizzy

driving my cart hard over rough stones
angering the course attendant and
the grey sky so dark even in midday
twilight all day disoriented rain drops

begin to fall then stop all at once as if unsure
or maybe just lacking necessary motivation.
I wrote a long email to my friend in Nebraska.
I had some kind of thesis about the world

being composed of posters and commenters.
My argument flagged before it could really
fall in sheets like the deluge paused on
a brink just beyond the horizon line.

A sponge violently wrung over the sink
then a damp gasp settling into a cold afternoon.

Kleptoparasite

sweat shining on yr chest
shoulders back upright jogging
shirtless and you smile nicely
at ladies pushing strollers

they mostly ignore ppl like you
within his own cloud the park maintenance
worker blows dust with a leaf blower
nothing can be permanent

the mind reels at the tiny stakes of life
the island-dwelling frigate bird snatches
chicks from nests of other seabirds
and no one cares at all

flowers drop from the branch
to make way for the fruit
you run thru city trails into sunlight
but outside the consciousness

of all those busy mothers walking
their babies on a lovely day
each one full of hope but scanning
the skies for red-throated frigate

Morning Bell

In the sunlight among the hedges
the red robin chases after the brown robin.
I see them dart from thick leaves
raked into piles along the edge of the lawn.

A garbage truck is emptying all the bins
along the neighborhood street and squirrels
avoid death beneath its wheels as they run
across the road. The spiraling earth is turning

again in the vacuum of space and my entire
consciousness exists in this green yard along
a boulevard just south of downtown in a medium
American city. The girls who I have loved

well, I hope they are also in the sunshine somewhere.
I hope they hope the same for me. I bought a gold
necklace with colored beadwork a strange and
almost grecian-seeming mezzaluna charm.

I don't know, it's just a silly trifle
but i will give it to my valentine tomorrow
along with a flower bouquet in a copper vase and
a card with an inscription from Rimbaud which reads:

"I have dreamed of the green night with dazzled snows
A kiss slowly rising to the eyes of the sea."

Materialism

"Who can say whether all these
lunches at the Vietnamese bistro
amount to anything
like a smoked mirror
they reflect less accurately
but are perhaps more lovely for it."

"Yes but all those aisles of tube socks
the necessary ephemera of life
sometimes I think only consumer products are real
everything else is just romanticism."

"Of course, but only
as the squirrel in his tree
is more concerned with movement of a leaf
than changes in the weather."

Wild Life

Given the blue sky and bright sun
all the green leaves twisting gently
in the breeze it seems impossible not
to be overcome by heart stopping anxiety

feels as if almost nothing in my life
is right or meaningful maybe it is the aluminum
in my brain from industrial society and i must
drink silica water to cleanse my body of heavy metals

maybe i have been drinking too much alcohol and
this is a type of delayed hangover mechanism
of subtle body chemistry the mourning dove go
from branch to ground and ground to branch

it doesn't seem as if there is any purpose really
the heart wants everything for a time and then
it wants everything to go away.

Au Revoir Les Enfants

medivac helicopter chops across
the city greenbelt canyons searching
for some unlucky rock climber fallen

into a hell among oaks and cedars
i carry my soft cooler down to the
river that runs thru the canyon heart

i saw a bunny step into my path
and stand motionless watching me
there was no sound for a few beats

then he returned to the bushes and
i continued walking down the ridge
toward the icy stream frothing below

balanced my softpack of cold drinks on a rock
while i dipped my body into a calmer eddy
chopper circles overhead but i lose track

of its position in the sky and then the sound
of its blades also phases out of my consciousness
i was born from the ether and my perception is limited

clouds move across the face of the sun and
hot light dusts my shoulders above the waterline
hundreds of tiny frogs small as grasshoppers

burst from a grass bank and tumble to rushing current

Swallow Flight

In the dark breath of night I saw a bird fly
over the steeple and dip sharply
down to the gravestones.

Light bit back away from the scene
and blue clouds closed in
I wanted so badly to know you.

Not that the earth
would pause for a moment.

3 *Home*

Main Street Marketplace

In suburban neighborhood communities
everyone is always looking to upgrade.
Divorce in the neighborhood is an

exciting event because both a new house
and a new spouse will be hitting the market.
Most new houses being built use nearly

every inch of buildable space often leaving
just little strips of grass or xeriscape
for the front and back yards.

This is because the resale value of a home
depends so much on the square footage.
Really, the whole thing

all of it

is just based on a simple mathematical formula.

You Can Count on Me

the drunken mess of my little brother
dragging him home in the night away
from the party he had become militantly

comical screaming in the faces
of other party guests and laughing
in a strangely glottal way i had never

really heard from him before
his breath humid with beer
and wet cigarette butts

his torn military jacket faded
from a once olive color into
an indefinite tan

i love him this is the brother i love

in the night on our walk back to my house
beneath streetlamps he rants about the supposed
superiority of the other people at the party

he keeps referring to it as their "excelsior"
he keeps repeating this but i'm not sure
exactly what he means and he wears

oversized plastic glasses you might see
on a bootcamp private in a war movie
his blonde hair is receding and wispy

i put my arm around him and squeeze
even as my senses recoil... i'm completely sober
he stops yelling and gives me a kiss

on the ear
missing my cheek
this brother who i love in the misty dark night

Alicia

today my love for you
is like a balloon blown up
really big but also

that isn't exactly what i want to say
i saw two squirrels playing in the lawn
and thought of you i saw

a squirrel on its hind legs
shelling and eating a pecan
with its little hands and

i thought of you

the sky is blue and it's sunny
this summer day and i will
ride my bike to work today

i put on a blue short-sleeve
collared shirt and my whiskers
are a little long and i felt excited

because i thought i looked handsome
i hoped you would think i look handsome
because i only experience myself

or at least my strongest perception of myself is
thru the lens of what you might be thinking about me
and i imagine what you might be thinking about me

all the time.

Amazon Prime Day

My little sister uses an oxygen mask.
It's not clear whether she really needs it.
Some suspect she conned the doctors into prescribing it.

She keeps a dog named Janet confined
to a chainlinked pen and it shits everywhere.
Janet lives in squalor but no one knows what to do.

The other dogs have the run of a large kennel but will try to kill
Janet if they can reach her and Janet is small.
She can't defend herself against larger dogs.

My sister lives in a single-wide trailer on my parent's land
with her husband and no one is allowed to enter her home.
Probably because she is a hoarder.

I go home for a barbecue and see from across the driveway
the overgrown entrance to my sister's house
and I see Janet in her pen.

We look away and talk about lunch.

April When I Remembered You

I had an argument with my wife because
She was criticizing everything about me.
But also I want to give you her perspective.

I said "you are being a jerk to me."
She said "don't call me a jerk" and later
She was most upset that I called her a jerk.

I sat in the rain and watched a soccer match.
Then I went to Red Lobster and it smelled funny.
But it was fine, I ordered a Sam Adams.

At home we watched the movie Tommy Boy
With the kids and I have to say it was very funny.
We all laughed alot on the sofa and later I thought

Too much about dead relatives who I loved so deeply.
And that changed things a bit because it's hard to maintain
Just the good vibes and any way kind of false to try.

I don't purport to know you at all.
I will tell you something true that I feel connected to you
No matter how far in time you may be from this moment.

I am typing in the dining area and drinking pinot noir.
I love you very much now.

To Anyone Who Ever Had a Heart

Sometimes it's all I have left
when everything else is a failure
no one likes my style but I can still
talk yer ear off about it

Ha! I could always talk yer ear off
just a big baby talker
like all the others

you would listen and I sensed
you loved me though never
mentioned it to anyone else
and lord knows it hasn't been easy

sometimes it was all I had
and still was nothing at all
just a sad sorry joke that you
might love me as I once loved you

in the living room it's sometimes
all I have left when I think so many
things, you know? Of course I'm getting
older but I still think so many things don't you?

Many Worlds

I suppose I ended up in this world
when our paths branched and you
went to the only place consciousness could take you
once entangled, we decohered
now our paths are further and further away
drifting down causeways whose origins are
already obscured.

But I always think when I am alone
that you will come tunneling back
across whatever barrier separates our multiverse
uncertainty alone suggests you may appear
and our particulate energies
will regroup in wave form
until caught unawares
viewed by the observer
we can finally return to the classical world.

II. THE UNMOVED MOVER

To start the lawnmower you pulled the cord
and it whipped back fast
the engine would not turn over it smelled like a gasoline leak
you taught me but I was too sloppy
I cried when the lawnmower cord
scorched your forearm

I remember the panic when we came home and you were not
    there.

I am getting smaller, younger
as you are growing bigger and stronger
your dayglo-colored newsboy hat
comic print shirt and soft eyes
I could have burst my chest could have burst
with pride when you drove me in your
dusty Nova and we smoked cigarettes.

I would ask you questions about science fiction
and you always gave me the whole story
there is no one like that left in this world
gravity decay, orbit faltered, came unmoored
the galaxy grew so old
that all its stars drifted apart.

The Farthest Mosque

smoking pot and marlboro reds with
the college prof who lives on my street
we're listening to yung thug's new mixtape
drinking beer he has a wonderful grassy lawn

a fantastic treehouse for his kids and
a chicken coop he built himself I'm going up
some kind of internal elevator the squirrels
are rampant on this sunny day we're talking

about the federal interest rate what is that line maybe
its biblical about all the works and days of hands
I'm sure I'm misremembering but I think
it seems important I've had too much beer

once again and I'm high and these cigarettes are
making me woozy I think the cigarettes make me
more fucked than anything else the evening
is coming very soon I'm rushing into something

I'm traveling very very fast into the night

The Center of the Page

Along the streets on the way home
walking past the gutters with their
still water and dark grackles shuddering
black wet feathers in passing headlights

sweeping across chainlink fence
impossible years of this walking
or just living in the city and
seeing everyday the garish colored

chain restaurants and handsome young
waiters working the sidewalk cafes
the elderly walkers who seem lost
but really just have nowhere to be.

I saw a policeman arresting a vagrant
and felt sorry for both of them the cold
air and their exhalations puffing into one
another the moon is just a space station.

Streetwise

When I was a teenager I worked at the corner store
there was a musician who stopped by for beer and cigarettes
his name was Streetwise it was his stage name but also

it was just what everyone called him he was middle aged
always carried his guitar he would hang flyers on the window
advertising his gigs at the nearby coffee shop the flyers said

"the more you drink the better I sound!"
I went to see him play and he was a blues musician
but he played things like nirvana covers in a blues style

it was interesting he was a nice happy guy I liked him though
he seemed lightly drunk all the time even in the mornings.
He would buy beer and cigarettes cracking jokes and laughing

with me and the other customers then he would go outside
to use the payphone seemed to call a woman you could hear him
enraged shouting at her calling her a cunt, a whore, all that stuff

then he would come back into the store smiling and laughing
joking asking me to break a dollar so he could get more quarters

go back outside

and use the payphone to call that lady again.

I Still Have Not Quit Smoking

March when all my mistakes accumulated
to that shadow fall
crazed with youth, boyhood I was mad
as a foaming dog for transcendent high
you were strong possessed
lovely as a dark well.

March desert journey
play in white sands new mexico
snowbound grand canyon
I knew I loved you when
you swallowed three joints at a DEA checkpoint.

If I could just speak plainly
I would say that I didn't know how to react.

If I have disappointed you or stayed too long
it was March that did me in.

Six Pack and a Bottle of Rosé

In the morning with the birds chirping
I caught my breath and exhaled 12 emails
typing on my phone garbage trucks outside
slamming dumpsters under round strawberry moon

a whole list of people waiting at the other end
for instructions like who knows really
Cleveland finally won a championship
but that didn't change anything in my life

Alicia says I'm drinking too much and yes
of course I am what do people do at night surely
the jellyfish floating off the shore have something
to entertain themselves after everyone else

has gone to bed when the phone is buzzing with
unwanted advances when the sky is clouded and
no stars are even visible at all and everyone is
talking and encroaching on your remaining pleasure.

Gucci Linens

flowered sheets crumpled around your feet
in the morning you feel fine today bright
windows all the little potted succulents
hardly need water at all empty cigarette

pack empty bottles whatever that sort of thing
the lunar space station crashing toward earth
live feed cams shutting off at inopportune moments
even those mad ideologies murderously circulating

the body the lungs the air outside people are stooped
looking at mobile phone devices perhaps there
is a new trend app release or news that something
elegant occurred something good for people maybe

but what do I know about any of it I saw
leaves unfolding in time lapse on television
watched fireworks from the elks lodge pool
fried whitefish dark beer and malt vinegar

the faint scent of reefer on the wind returned home muddy
        headed
laughing and drank more wine watched mike tyson's
greatest knockouts and bo jackson career highlights
fell asleep to awake in flowered sheets laughing to myself

Force Majeure

a tree crashed from my yard
through my neighbor's fence smashed
their deck and fell into their pool

act of god I told them what can be done
but they were sullen and wanted to talk
about insurance claims and liabilities

the husband wore his shirt unbuttoned
on his exposed hairy chest he seemed
to be wearing some sort of snake medallion

the wife was a nice college professor lady
just had her first baby quite late in life
she seemed bewildered and reserved

we stood on their deck surveying the damage
the pool now dyed dark green from the leafy
treetop soaking at the bottom of the deep end

really a very pleasant day a mourning dove
strutted beside the fallen tree looking for beetles
a cool breeze rippled across the pool surface

the murky green water like some forest pond
I took a deep breath and exhaled slowly
act of god I said shaking my head act of god

Intercession of Pope Leo I

Tensions when the bottle of wine
ran out and it wasn't clear whether another
would be opened or things really could
continue as they had been at all after

so many botañas at the restaurant watching
copa américa matches on the broken TV
hanging over the bar that sort of thing you know
times when contemporary life seemed to call for

one more uncorking one more dice roll or what
have you the eternal sunset the eternal shootout
violent end to a night that began with crème de menthe
and soft kisses over frutas del mar the moon moving

subtly closer sneaking up like whoa I didn't notice
things at all I thought the world I already comprehended
would stay like this forever seemed only natural
my hands my brain all I can really bring to the table.

The queen of violet city sat on her camp chair fiery
fingertips manicured nails pointing at exactly what
she wanted while the rest of us swooned and held
tight to comforting notions of personal superiority

somehow we would prevail somehow this thing would
work itself out to a favorable conclusion she looked
away and it was like a string running from her lips to
my chest had been stretched taut then snapped.

87

I sat woozy staring at the wine fridge so many choices
directions like the sack of Rome I could accept my tribute
and leave or burn the damn place down salt the earth reboot

western civilization or whatever.

Jerusalem

Recent news items include a soccer star
indicted for tax fraud geopolitical dissolution
babies falling into gorilla pens

red moon rising on the summer solstice
the death of a number of patriarchs
the ongoing recreation of structures

meant to define otherwise random events
holographic stage rapping at a concert
for all the kids who can afford tickets

in Jerusalem daily life is sometimes interrupted
with violence but everywhere is sometimes violent
death feels more random than ever before

the lottery aspects of life seem to have intensified
to a degree that threatens the concept of free will
ants work their way up from the yard into the house

rats move into the crawlspace above the ceiling
a carafe of wine designed to aerate the wine to cause
chemical changes that may or may not exist or even matter.

Data Center

The new painted bike lanes bright white
and yellow in the sun the allergic pollen
heavy air and cut grass clippings drying
in neat rows all the henchmen of industry

puttering around living rooms checking iphone
updates social movement hashtags political party
editorials stooges upon stooges the night before
the sphinx in egypt rested on its forequarters

as it always does in the dry sand born in the desert
like all wild, ambitious things possessed of the knowledge
the horror of empty spaces but in this oak lined neighborhood
the bike lanes are carefully striped away the electric

hybrid vehicles are silent as fish the moon is not real
it's a space station everything serves some ulterior
purpose conspiracy theories are of course fake because
they are meant to obscure truth there is more insect life

on this planet measured in biomass than all of humanity
last night we watched the wine swirl and aerate into a carafe
we read books about a privileged kind of desperation
we checked our phones we stared into that blue light

until it suffused our dreams and there was no border
no boundaries whatsoever.

New Year 2016

At the poolside bar I ordered two whiskeys
on New Year's Eve bummed a cigarette from
the bartender told him I resolved to quit

he thought that was funny I smoked furtively
my kids were swimming in the pool and probably
saw me smoking after so many lessons about

the dangers of cigarettes imagine their confusion but
also think of my own confusion nothing makes sense
after all this shabby hotel populated by budget travelers

from foreign countries cheap but close to the theme park
its pink paint peeling a reminder not really of better times
but just that no one cared anymore it wasn't important

happy New Year I smoked that cigarette drank one
of the whiskeys gave the other to my wife and
resolved to do something different that would maybe

create a different outcome tried but couldn't manage
to stay up late enough to watch the fireworks they
launched and exploded aimlessly in the sky while I slept

and plastic cocktail cups littered the pool area in the morning
some unlucky maintenance man gathering them slowly
in the fog no hurry at all there's a whole new year ahead.

Suzie Orman

hey this a poem abt how I bought
a house figured some of you poetry
ppl maybe would want to know abt that

I just worked one summer when my wife
also had a job and we lived off her income
banked mine then we had a few thousand
dollars for a down payment

actually only put 5% down to be honest
and imma tell you I am someone
who rented many a shithole
in my life I worked call centers
and pizza kitchens all the time

owning a house is better
its so much better bc rent
cant be increased and you dont
gotta fuck with the landlord and theres

other shit too taxes and stuff
this is a poem abt practical advice

September

On a saturday things seem fine
especially if the sun is out then
I feel as if problems are temporary

harmless really the autumn comes
maybe I attend a football game drinking
brown beer from cans in koozies

all the marauders relax take a break
the problems of existence its many fees
that seem perpetual midnight crush

the dark remembrance I don't see that anymore
it's just crickets jumping out of grass
ahead of my footsteps pretty young girls

riding bikes toward the pool soon humanity
will be perfectible the weekend in autumn
won't be such an isolated event my hair will

grow long it won't matter the crisis will
dissolve like margarita salt drifting toward
the bottom of the drink.

Levelland

love at least might be something
different but sure didn't seem likely
in west texas where you may not know
this but it stinks like literal shit pretty
much all the time from natural gas

or something and the old timers wear
cowboy hats and say stuff like mmmm
smells like money and I guess
they think that is clever and another
thing you may not know about west texas

pretty much nothing grows the place is dry
and flat and the ground is cracked so
just tumbleweeds and scraggly brush

so no it didn't seem particularly likely that
love might find someone here unless you
are crazy fucking churchy or something
a weirdo basically by any rational standard
and you praised god and enjoyed the smell

of shit so when nothing grows from nothing
you can't act surprised

Fox News

my friend shoots guns
he thinks he cant trust
CNN bc they never show
good stories abt ppl using guns

he loves stories about navy seals
and special ops in general
or old men gunning down teenagers
who had been attacking them

he was a nurse but he married
a surgeon and now he doesnt work
anymore he manages investment
properties owned by the surgeon

he shoots his guns and
builds furniture in his garage

Beauty is Unknown

We had a garden party
with vegan appetizers
lots of poets showed up
to read about psychosexual love
internet absurdity
and the death of art.

As it got late
I was drunk and smoking cigarettes
the younger poets sipped club sodas
they seemed brave and self-aware

I heard darkness as the sun set
insufficient light
felt as though
I were facedown in mud
but when I looked toward the fenceline
I saw

the wisteria yet dropt its blooms!

Marriage Anniversary

A mystery how we ended up here
every night we go to sleep
and wake in the morning
somehow that process
brought us to this home
married with young children
claiming to be ours.

We were young children!
I think we still are.
Having slept and awakened
are we so changed?

Oh how time carried us gently
as a mother carries her cubs.
I loved you as a girl
and you are a girl to me still
though I fear
that same beast of time
now stalks us for the kill.

On the Occasion of My 37th Birthday

there is a lady in my workout class who is always
smiling and nodding at me and sometimes when
I'm getting water after class I come back to my
stuff and she has already put away my weights

and so when she walks by I thank her but
she just smiles and walks away and then I go outside
and get on my bike to ride home she waves at me from
her car and I try to wave back while steering with

my other hand then it's sunny outside and I take the
longer trail home across the ped bridge over the lake
there is a canoe access point and it's like a U shaped
concrete slope where the bike trail crosses over

it's a perfect half pipe so if no joggers are in the way
I speed up and catch a little air over the lip but if
people are jogging or pushing strollers I'm cautious
and pass carefully I congratulate myself on that.

I ride the bike trail all the way up the street to my house
after exercise class and I know I'm getting older all the time
but I can inhale the fall oxygen and exhale slowly and
feel certain I'm just as young as I ever have been and

all those sad things that have happened to me are mistakes
maybe they were meant to happen to someone else, I don't know.

Next Year's Glossy Magazines

glossy magazines spilled across my coffee table
outside the window I can see the grass will recover
from last summer's drought
now that winter is tailing off

I am older and still unworthy
having escaped death for another year
through no merit of my own

all the saints are also one year older
in their graves

on the deck we have arrayed three chairs around an iron table
and there is a miniature camp-style chair for my daughter
while the adults tend the grill and drink beers
she wears sunglasses and sips an arnold palmer

I don't know if there is anything beyond the veil
or if we will ever, finally, understand

nothing seems likely to be better than this

though I have seen poets whose beauty was already celestial
snuffed young by that insentient philistine
I am content to be dull and living

I want to read next year's glossy magazines
delight in some meaningless fashion trend
watch the grass return to bare patches

see my daughter grow too large for her dino-print camp chair
and sit with the half-drunk adults
to sing sweetly off-key
while I play clumsy guitar

Sober Day

saturday and I'm not drinking today
in the garden little birds flit back
and forth from the fence to the dirt

neurotically pointlessly the sky is blank
a rusted iron pole holds a basketball goal
teetering from its screws and the drunks

next door sip vodka in the mornings
the gardener runs his leaf blower beneath
my bedroom window this is my only day

so I object to this treatment there are laws
no one can go on like this forever

Lost in Space

My son has been jogging with me after work.
We have been going almost four miles a day.
Even though he is only nine years old
He has endless enthusiasm for these runs.

When we return home it seems he could easily
Set right back out for another run.
He texts me when I am at work and
Encourages me to hurry home.

As I grow softer around the middle
I have only my will to endurance which
Has been practiced and hardened over years
Of interminable tasks until eventually

One realizes that a four mile run is pleasant
Because so much of life is harder to endure.
My son is all new energy bursting to speed
Out the front door and down the street.

He doesn't run to get fit or slow old age
Or because it gives him a break from work
But only to be outdoors and moving across
A completely unexplored planet.

Last Swim at Roberta's House

Bought my daughter goggles and a snorkel
gave it to her on my lunch break
but had to go back to work
while my wife was taking the kids
to the neighbor's pool

my daughter said
come with us dad
Roberta is moving
it's the last time
we'll swim in her pool

didn't know what to say she was so
lovely and her message
seemed true and urgent

I watched them walk away
she waved to me with her snorkel
mask I bought it for her
and now I have to
go back to work.

4 *Dreams*

Six Seeds

along the banks of the murky river
we watched a lunatic pitbull knockover
the trashcan spilling bottles and cans
a surly couple cleaned the mess

we walked through the statuary and discussed AI poetry
we considered deep meaning and the connections
that exist faintly at the periphery of understanding
whether an intelligent machine can discern that nexus

white limestone dust powdered my blanket
we removed sticker burrs together and
you taught me to fold it "envelope style"
you think a planned economy might be good

in the graveyard we search for minor
historical figures among the mausoleums
so bright and hot with nowhere to sit
what is the meaning after all of the mural

painted on the side of an oldtimey drug store
it depicts a boxer standing atop a defeated alien
you told me its message was unwelcoming
but of course we had not understood that

and so this city needs someone like you
you must stay with us at least
six months

She Judged Petals in Disarray

Riven to her downy bed
where lately lay her sleepy head
locks across the pillow white
dawn emerging out of night.

The night before she met a man
he offered up his able hand
and took her round to city lights
like others neither wrong nor right.

So she slept that night alone
asleep in dreams of pink sea foam
idly wondered if he might call
tho felt she did not care at all.

It wasn't that her heart was cold
for lit with life she was reckless, bold
but in her pyjamas lying there
love seemed like some rocky pier.

Where one might idle all alone
'neath the nightlamps twinkle shone
watch the waves with hope to happen
await the return of a lost sea captain.

Phoenicia

10,000 years of living in central
valleys the phoenicians had no
word for transistors they only
spent time thinking abt strange gods

phoenician sailors made it all the way
up the coast pretty far farther than
previous sailors had gone they
knew abt the zodiac and sometimes

painted their faces they could fly
helicopters but only theoretically
they had children who would never
pay attention when their parents
were trying to teach them things

a famous phoenician poet
wrote alot abt his neighbor who was
an asshole apparently he invented rhyme
to describe his neighbors speech impediment

he had seen the sun go down beneath
mediterranean waves burning more blue
than any hdtv could realistically portray
he once ate a tiny octopus found
alive snagged in his fishing net

This One

heart when you stopped and then confusion
everywhere abt how to continue I did love you
and then you died in that way death makes ppl

so permanently gone it feels absurd that nothing
can be done abt it this is what ppl mean when they
say they woke from a dream thinking you were alive again

not that a miracle had occurred really but that some
mistake had been corrected not much different than if
your credit card was stolen but you called the bank

and everything was fixed and then it was ok
and thats the damn unbelievable thing abt death
its really real the clouds roll across the daytime sky

rosemary grows and you smell it when you rub yr fingers
across its blades dumb ppl smart ppl mingle freely
in the crowds in the spiraling whirlpool of heedless

ungoverned circumambulations but you are gone and I'm afraid
its not just some administrative error the physics of the universe
didnt allow for you to continue and god is just trying out

formulas the results are like waves they keep washing into shore
and nothing would ever change that and maybe no one really
would even want to

IRL

Mary in the night it feels like we're together
like your flat stomach and my hand met like two
humans could understand one another like the waterpark

rides where you slide down the runway toward the bottom
dunk under the waves and felt happy to die there why not
Mary why not anything linguine with littleneck clams

that sort of thing and heartbreak I felt everything for you
your online machinations beautiful because of their futility
the tweets and updates hahaha who could ever care about

any of it about nighttime when the stars hid we all
knew something was up and it wasn't just the drugs this time

felt like a new moon Mary felt like irish independence finally
felt like something terrible was born that night the smell
of drunken thai shrimp in late night cafes tiger beer

in a frosted mug and Mary you would not think it was
interesting or funny at all you have over a thousand followers
on whatever website is au courant hahaha and the jasmine

flowered on your birthday anyway but it seemed you were
snapping or instagramming the pics I didn't know really
couldn't say when I was endlessly helplessly in love with you

Drunk Dials at 330am I Love Them

you can do anything you want to
sometimes you sleep late
smoke pot in the morning
but thats ok because I know
it makes you happy to wear

that black and white checkered
marilyn monroe print t-shirt
with no bra and I can see
the river jordan and even that

far shore all the cages opened
all my people free to roam
long legs just a bit unshaved
nighttime smile you are

smoking pot again youve
been doing it all day but
thats alright you can do
anything you want to

The Good Wine

the good wine and these certain
habits ppl exhibit preening
almost unnoticed and in the
mirror they catch a glimpse

some other life across choppy waters
salty clams shelled from the brine
and darkbeer on a grey sky day
white boats slipping into rainy

harbor the good wine Madeline
your back arched just a bit
white crocheted top thrown over
your dark eyes moving across

the water like a gull had we been
here before Madeline why did I feel
as though we had always been talking
at a cafe on a rainy cold day Madeline

you ordered the good wine and we shared
briny clams the black beers I drank
made me too full the sky so stupid
and benevolent and grinning

through its clouds and the red
surface of mars could not have
been so desolate so windswept as
that casual hand through your hair

III

and those eyes skipping across
rough waters madness all around

Because Our Hearts Are Human and Beautiful

i know what i see is a false peak the true peak
lies just beyond that ridge but we can pause
in the shadow of this rock among the dust

if such a pretty lady as you can't make it here
well what about me then? a disaster obviously
lacking those saffron colored heart beams

the night mistresses haunt forgotten graveyards
that tuneless cipher the midnight revolutionaries
did you ever really understand the wheeling city skies?

ash tray sitting directly in front of a pride of barbados
which is opening itself to the sun in such a suggestive
manner my glasses fog and get slippery on my nose

it's obviously frightening to stand at the base of a skyscraper
or even in a window at the top of a skyscraper
do you depend on others, like me?

and other weaknesses we can discuss
at your leisure

Not Abt That Life

a human dog was living
underwater as best it could
mammals have returned to the sea before

oh fine said dog even if things are sandy
people travel so far to the beach
why not live there everyday

human dog saw urchins and krill
wondered abt physics could it be
a profession can anyone really

do what they love is there something
abt the physical forces of the universe
that dictate giant whales must eat tiny krill

the oceanfloor was so quiet
good for talks like that

human dog was too fragile for the
abovesea life not abt that life

Reverse Photosynthesis

There are trees that grow only in dark patches
of the earth so they are easy to miss
if you arent paying attention

I filtered their dark shadow
you professed not to care
and we were alone leaning on our shadow trees

a stream in the shade passed through
watered the night drinker
returned the scaly bark to its
lonely state scared of the sun

scared of photosynthesis
the breeze in the dark space
enlivened the shadow tree
four ministers
baptized the tree at each corner

sprinkled water at its base and you cooed
among its branches
so too the shadow of the earth
fed your ecliptic want

The Sitting Room

There is an upholstered chair
reserved for our special guest
when she sits in that chair
she can see through four windows
and if you sit across from that chair
you can see the honored guest.

At nighttime our guest grows pale
she sips strong drinks and seems to sink
lower in her seat her long hair
falls around her face
ere the glow from porchlight
does softly illumine.

And in the daytime our guest in
sun refracted through beveled glass
rainbow bedeck her collared blouse
she is attentive to the sounds of starlings
and ivy climbing windows.

American Werewolf in Prague

I was trying to meet up with you
but my phone buzzed; I lost my head
ran into a friend
from school

there were people everywhere in the park
talking with me and making me late

I read an email by the fountains
the day was not yet hot

later we had wine on the back deck
we are werewolves but never transform
my heart is always
a full moon.

Discounts are Discussed in Person

new york high line converted into a garden and we
weren't cynical about that we were happy to walk thru
those shrubs to be eye level with a yoga class in a highrise

to understand the work that actors put into a performance
baring their bodies and trying but not always succeeding
to tell you something about how they think and perceive

what nighttime walks feel like to them what their
mom said in the backyard that was strangely lasting
over drinks nice punches and peach infusions clinking

ice cubes and white teeth when Sharon laughed I could see
her incisors like fangs so dark and inviting in that kind of
desperate way nothing good comes of that I guess but

we also have to consider that nothing good

really

comes from refusing that

Content Creators

Winsome when you beckoned
my face in my hands
latent signals drifting down from the heavens
blue stones along our gravel path
hand in hand
mostly silent

though you did point to orions belt
traced its line down toward a house
seemed abandoned
seemed concerned with exterior thoughts
my head, your head
broadcasting signals
back to that intergalactic waystation.

Paradise

in paradise there are no bosses
no difference between people
who arrive with good intentions
sunshine is important but not

necessary beaches are alcohol-free
that might surprise you and in paradise
animals are afforded some basic rights
at least helicopters don't patrol but

they are available for rides all the people
living and dead remain committed to experiencing
nothing painful at all ever again at nighttime
in paradise there are still problems or at least

thoughts of problems and if I find myself
lying awake in paradise thinking of all
the problems of the old world or this one
it doesn't mean I want to return to the dark

Young Once Only

Streets were littered with gaping yokels
maundering lit cabarets
shine a sheen on the pavement
ducked you into a shot bar
and we gulped noisy drinks

stumbled back across the sidewalk
careening against ill-suited popinjays
you buried your face beneath my coat
laughed and smeared mascara

guided you in my arm
toward a quiet side street
wiped your eyes
lit cigarettes and strolled slowly

at the foot of a high-rise
led you down a few short steps
opened the door
to a late night Thai cafe

you brushed long hair from the sides of your face
blinking in the lights you
realized after morning
we would never see one another again.

Chrysanthemums

On your scooter
gunning the turn
I held you tight
"Cherie" you would say
and I shuddered and you called me
the meadow lark.

We ducked under ocean waves
to rest on the seafloor
you would keep me
in green light filtering
down from the abandoned surface.

But church bells rang
and woke us to a
hushed wedding
on our knees
we vowed never to grow old.

You bought me a dress
from the thrift store
I worried about the spirit
of a dead former owner
but you loved to take it off me
and after americanos in the morning
we turned the earth
on the chrysanthemums.

American Werewolf in Montreal

In my 34th year I became a werewolf
and I suppose everything changed
the computer screens were gibberish
I did not recognize
glowing screens

no more sonnets, no more peach trees
if none of it mattered as much as
an image macro if cherry blossoms fell
upon some soft cheek in the lamplight

no mercy for me a creature like that
should be put down if nothing else
out of a sense of decency

My Poor Mind's Out of Tune

Horse lamps lit feathers on the ground
mud slopped the water's edge
sulphuric notes on the breeze
red sky at morning red sky at night
my eyes were blotted out.

We took a carriage ride through the city streets
drove like that until morning
plotting a course by vermilion stars.

In the winter we always stay indoors
the tree branches are bare
anyway, exotic birds migrate to our living room.

Talking about the intransigence of blood relations
as though I couldn't hear every word
I bought you native american turquoise
you bought me a bottle of good scotch.

We always stay indoors in the winter
and in the spring
it's time for school again
are we children or parents this time?

Deranged as though
the summerheat melted polar ice caps
reversed the magnetic poles
flooded your mind with
thoughts of the luxembourg gardens.

Will you return to stroll those gardens with me in the fall?
Afterward we can watch american movies at the cinema.

Lubbock

clara lee you faltered
it all became too much
if life was just like dating
we were always going dutch

your spirit high and noisome
I shuddered in the hall
put you on a pedestal
tho hoping you might fall

if ice is on the branches
no stream is in the brook
I never took my chances
you cried so hard you shook

but still we are so hopeful
while snow is on the ground
has anybody ever left
this godforsaken town?

Three Penny Opera

mania taking over the leaves
in piles on the ground now wrecked
branches from the storm even in the eye

of jupiter these winds could not carry
my heavy heart back to where we met
the circles form and dissolve

mention one old convenience store clerk
many years behind the counter now selling
vapes and vape accessories to boys with pimples

its really true they say aliens are visiting
we tune into their frequency like a radio dial
the sun rises over the pyramids of tikal

the sun sets at chichen itza illuminating
a snake that travels down the temple steps
vendors sell jaguar trinkets and panther calls

the waitress has blue hair at our restaurant
she tells me it is good and profitable to be a firefighter
i think it is good to have iced tea with plenty of ice

and the solar eclipse reveals the shape of the earth

Rebel Rebel

Winthrop Chester moved through fields of love
massachusetts colony doldrums to chesapeake bay
mysteries little crabs working their way up from
sandy holes.

He wore the black uniform
white neckpiece
ate regular meals of corn
and partially rendered lamb grease.

He never felt a human touch
except on certain sanctified occasions
his body an inviolate temple
a shrine to some infinitely demanding
goddess and poor Winthrop
her henpecked saint.

But he knew that salty
air and the fecund odor of
the seaside on an overcast day
were alchemy and that promises of an afterlife
were, at best, beside the point.

And then to make his home among the seagulls
to reject the church and society and the safety of backward
    promises.

Winthrop shed all his debts and wore his skin
like a horse hair shirt.

128

Night Storm

Nightfall and called me back
to that dark rainstorm
it's all trouble
for the possum living in the crawlspace
the wet leaves drip

pierces that water and sleeps

I saw a man in the shadows
dip down to the culvert
seemed he thought I missed him
in his black dress and wide brimmed hat

this night the car headlights spot my journey
the flood rages through the drainage ditch
I'm trapped again in the storm sewer
and the water level rises

this night there are black birds on the front porch
shaking their feathers

I was born to walk through rainy nights
I was born to take that hiding man
by his blistered hand

until trash like us
is washed from the asphalt.

About the Author

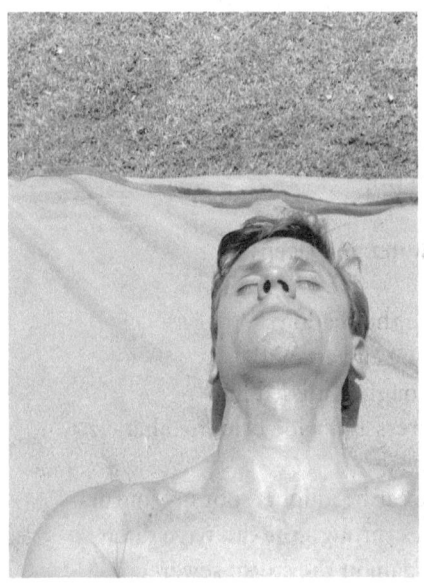

WALLACE BARKER lives in Austin, Texas. *Collected Poems* is his second book. His debut collection, *La Serenissima*, was published by Gob Pile Press. More of his work can be found at wallacebarker.com

Also from Maximus Books
YOU, THE VIEWER AT HOME, MOON
by Tom Will

SO WHAT?
by Hayden Church

DECAY NEVER CAME (*coming soon*)
by David Kuhnlein

www.ingramcontent.com/pod-product-compliance
Lightning Source LLC
Chambersburg PA
CBHW011230120626
46549CB00008B/3209